CFA LEVEL 1: 2026 FIXED INCOME

Complete in just 1-Week

Dr. M. Imran Ahsan Dhothar

Copyright © 2026 M. Imran Ahsan

All rights reserved

The characters and events portrayed in this book are fictitious. Any similarity to real persons, living or dead, is coincidental and not intended by the author.

No part of this book may be reproduced, or stored in a retrieval system, or transmitted in any form or by any means, electronic, mechanical, photocopying, recording, or otherwise, without express written permission of the publisher.

Printed in the United States of America

To all smart learners

Investing is the art of managing risk, not avoiding it.

PETER LYNCH

CONTENTS

Title Page
Copyright
Dedication
Epigraph
Preface
Learning Module 1   1
Learning Module 2   4
Learning Module 3   9
Learning Module 4   13
Learning module 5   21
Learning Module 6   25
Learning module 7   29
Learning Module 8   33
Learning module 9   35
Learning Module 10   40
Learning Module 11   43
Learning Module 12   45
Learning Module 13   48
Learning Module 14   50
Learning module 15   54
Learning module 16   56

Learning module 17   60
Learning module 18   62
Learning Module 19   66

PREFACE

Fixed Income 2026— A Concise Guide to Success
Want to pass the CFA Level 1 exam in the most effective and efficient manner? Look no further. This book tends to provide one with complete and concise information for clarity about the fixed income syllabus.
The aim of the book is to make complex concepts simple and easy to understand. It is our vision to distribute high-quality educational material at an affordable price. So far, this is our fourth book in the series, and we further plan an extension to cover all three levels of the CFA examination.

This book is all you need to ace the fixed-income concepts. We have used very simple language and structured it well to help you get a good grip on the content quickly and with minimal effort. We are confident that you will be able to complete this part of the CFA curriculum in a week.

Please send us your feedback and constructive criticism. Your feedback will help us serve you better in subsequent editions of this book.

Now, as we enter the fixed-income domain, let the journey to your CFA success begin!

Feel free to contact
Email: Ch.imranahsen@gmail.com

LEARNING MODULE 1

Fixed-Income Instrument Features

1: Describe the features of a fixed-income security

The most commonly referred fixed income security is bond, so when we talk about fixed income security, you can see it as a bond. A bond is a debt instrument that promises to pay a certain amount of cash at specific intervals to the lender by the issuer in the future. The issuer of the bond is the borrower, while the purchaser of the bond is the lender of funds.

The value of a bond is affected mainly by two things, the interest rate and risk associated with the bond issuer. When the interest rate rises, the bond's value goes down as the promised future cash inflows from that bond are discounted with a higher discount rate now.

The risk of default also affects the bond's value. The higher the risk, the lower the value of that bond. With higher default risk investors need more return in order to justify their investment.

A bond has the following features
- Name of the issuer of the bond
- Maturity date
- Par value (principal value)
- Coupon rate (interest rate to be paid)
- Currency of payments

Issuers of bond: The following can be the issuer of the bond
<u>Companies:</u> Financial and non-financial companies issue bonds.
<u>Sovereign governments (countries):</u> Countries also issue treasury

bills and other types of bonds.
Non-sovereign governments (municipalities, states, provinces)
Quasi-government entities: Bonds issued by government-sponsored agencies and entities.
Supranational entities: Global organizations like the European Union, IMF, etc.

Maturity: It is the date mentioned on the face of the bond on which the principal amount would be paid back. The period remaining in maturity is called tenor or term to maturity. Bonds with *maturity of less than one year are called money market securities,* and bonds with *maturity of more than one year are called capital market maturities.* Some bonds are issued with no maturity called *perpetual bonds*. In this type of bond, the principal amount is never paid back, but periodic payments are made forever.

Par value: The principal amount that would be paid at maturity is called par value. It also has different names like face value, maturity value, and redemption value. Face value can be identical to or different from the bond price. When a bond is traded or sold at a higher than-par value, it is called the premium. When face value is higher than the traded price, it is called a discount. Usually, the price is written (for the first issue) as a percentage of the face value.

Coupon rate: Coupon rate is the annual percentage rate of the face value. A bond with a face value of 100$ and a coupon rate of 10% will be paying 10$ annually. Bonds can be annual, semiannual, or quarterly paying. If the coupon rate is 10% in semiannual bond it would be paying 10%/2 = 5% after six months.

Currency: The currency in which the bond is issued is also mentioned on the bond's face. A *dual-currency bond is a bond in which the interest is being paid in one currency while the* principal is to be paid in another currency. Currency-option-bond gives the lender an option to choose from two currencies.

2: Describe the contents of a bond indenture and contrast affirmative and negative covenants

The legal contract between the issuer and buyer of a bond is called bond indenture or trust deed. Bond indenture specifies the responsibilities of the issuer and buyer and the characteristics of the bond. The provisions in the bond indentures are called bond covenants. These covenants are positive and negative.

Positive covenants: These are also called affirmative covenants. These are the actions that the borrower (issuer) promises to perform. Affirmative covenants usually include the promise to timely pay interest and principal amount, maintain a specific asset, and comply with applicable laws.

Negative covenants: These are the restrictions imposed on the issuer (borrower). These usually include restrictions on the sale or pledging of the same collateral asset and restrictions on additional borrowings. These covenants protect the bondholder's interests and reduce the default risk of the borrower.

LEARNING MODULE 2

Fixed-Income Cash Flows and Types

1: Describe common cash flow structures of fixed-income instruments and contrast cash flow contingency provisions that benefit issuers and investors

According to the payment structure, bonds can be divided into the following types.

Bullet structured bond/ Bullet bond: This is the most common type of bond. In this bond, the coupon payments are made periodically, and the principal amount is paid at maturity, usually along with the final coupon payment. For example, a three-year bond with a 100$ face value and coupon payment of 10% annually would pay as follows

Year	1	2	3
Payment	10	10	110

Fully amortized loan: When the bond pays the periodic coupon plus a proportion of the principal amount periodically, that is called a fully amortized loan. Car and home loans are usually fully amortized loans. This loan is fully amortized with the final payment, and there is no separate principal amount payment.

Partially amortized loan: This is not a very common type of fixed-income instrument. In this, some principal amount is amortized and paid along with coupon payment periodically, but at maturity, the unamortized amount plus coupon payments are made.

Contingency provisions

These are embedded options for either the issuer or holder of the bond. These provisions give the holder and or issuer some rights to exercise. (A bond with no contingency provisions is called a straight or option-free bond). Bonds with these embedded options can be callable, putable, or convertible bonds.

Callable bonds: Callable bonds give the right of <u>call option</u> to the bond issuer. The call option gives the right to the issuer to redeem a bond at a specific price at some specific date. It protects the issuer from risk of declining interest rate. For example a bond with 100$ face value and 5% coupon rate can have following type of call options;
The bond can be redeemed by issuer at 101% of face value on 21 January 20x3.
The bond can be redeemed by issuer at 100% of face value on 21 February 20x4.
If the issuer sees a huge decline in interest rate below than 5% he can redeem his bond at these two dates. That bond before any redeemable date is called *call protected* bond of that before period.
Companies also exercise call option (along with decline in interest rate) because their credit rating has increases and default risk is declined. Now, they can issue a new security with a coupon rate.
This callable option is not beneficial for the bondholder because this option will only be exercised when the market interest rate has fallen, and the investor will not get that much yield on any other instrument in the market. That's why callable bonds are issued with higher coupon rate in comparison to non-callable similar bonds. The difference between callable and non-callable identical bonds is equal to the value of the call option to the issuer. The call options can be any of the following types.
<u>American-style call option:</u> The call option can be exercised any time after the first call date.
<u>European style call option:</u> Bonds can be called only on specified date.
<u>Bermuda-style call option:</u> Bonds can be called on a specified date

after the first call date.
These call prices make the upper limits of the bond's price.

There is another call provision called the make-whole call provision.
Make-whole call provision: In this call provision, the issuer does not fix the call price, but the call price is calculated as the present value of the remaining coupon payments of that bond. The present value cannot be lower than the market value of that bond, so the issuer does not exercise this option unless there is an acquisition, merger, or similar type of thing happening with the issuer.

Putable bonds: The put option gives the right to the bondholder to sell back the bond to the issuer at a specific price. Just like the call option, the put option can be used but only by the bondholder. Bondholders will exercise the put option if the market or fair value of a bond is less than the put price or the credit rating of the issuer has fallen. As a putable bond gives extra rights to the bondholders in comparison to option-free bonds, that's why the putable bonds are sold at higher prices (or with lower yields) than option-free bonds with similar qualities.

Convertible bond: Convertible bond gives the right to bondholders to convert it with a specific number of common shares. When the market or fair value of the common shares increases, the bondholders can exercise this option. Again, this is beneficial for the bondholder, so the price is higher (lower yield). The convertible bonds are called hybrid security because of this convertible option into common shares. This gives minimum price protection to bondholders. *The conversion price* is the price at which bonds can be converted into common shares. *The conversion ratio is equal to the par value of the* bond/conversion price. *The conversion price is the market value of the common shares which are exchanged with bonds.*

Warrants: Warrants are not embedded options. They are given with straight bonds. Warrants give the right to bondholders to buy a company's shares at a given price over a period of time. Warrants attached to bonds are called sweeteners because they make a debt more attractive to the investors (with potential additions to the profits).

Contingent convertible bonds (CoCos): These are the bonds that will be converted into a specific number of common shares if a certain incident occurs. For example, a bond is issued with a condition to maintain a certain level of equity. If the equity falls below the required level, the bonds will be automatically converted into common shares to maintain that required equity level. This conversion will increase the equity and reduce the debt liabilities.

2: Describe how legal, regulatory, and tax considerations affect the issuance and trading of fixed-income securities

The bonds are subject to specific regulatory and tax laws depending upon where bonds are issued, traded, and where the bondholders are. According to geographic location, bonds can be divided into the following forms.

Domestic bonds: Bonds issued by domestic firms traded in the domestic market in local currency are called domestic bonds. For instance, if a US firm issues bonds that are traded in the US bond market in USD, they are called domestic bonds.

Foreign bonds: Bonds issued by a firm in another market in foreign currency and are being traded in that country are referred to as foreign bonds. For example, a US firm issues bonds in China, denominated in Yuan, and are being traded in China are called foreign bonds.

Euro bonds: Bonds issued outside of a country and denominated in currency other than the currency of the country where they are being traded are called Euro bonds. These bonds are subject to fewer regulations than domestic bonds. These bonds were initially started in Europe. That's why they are called euro bonds, and they can be in any currency (not necessarily in euro). Euro bonds are issued in bearer form. A bearer form is in which the bondholder is the owner. There is no need to register the name of the holder of that bond. The opposite of a bearer bond is a registered bond in which the name of the bondholder must be registered. Investors who want to avoid taxes hold bearer bonds.

Global bond: When a bond is issued in several countries at the same time that is called a global bond. This bond is also not denominated in the issuing country's currency.

Income from these bonds is taxed like other incomes. The capital gain is also taxed differently in different countries. Capital gain in the short term can be taxed differently or in the same way as long-term capital gain. Some bonds, like US municipal bonds, are exempted from tax.

In some jurisdictions, a discounted bond is treated as capital gain and taxed accordingly. Tax treatments also differ whether the bond is at a premium, discount, or par.

LEARNING MODULE 3

Fixed-Income Issuance and Trading

1: Describe fixed-income market segments and their issuer and investor participants

The global bond market can be divided with respect to the type of issuer, creditworthiness, maturity of bond, coupon structure, geography of issuance, indexing and taxability.

Classification with respect of issuer

There are three bond market sectors in his regard: government and government-related bonds, corporate bonds, and structured (securitized) bonds. Government and government related sector includes the bonds issued by federal government, state, municipal corporations and supranational organizations like World Bank. Corporate bonds are issued by *financial corporations* and issued by *non-financial corporations.*

With *securitized bonds* different debt products are pooled together to make a new security and then this security is sold to investors. These bonds are issued by special purpose entity (SPE) which is created for the issuance of these securities.

Classification with respect to the credibility of issuer

Credit rating is provided by credit rating agencies like Standard and poor's (S&P), Moody's and Fitch. According to S&P and Fitch AAA, AA and BBB are investment grade bonds. According to Moody's Aaa to Baa3 are the investment grade bonds. The bonds rated below than these grades are high yielding yet riskier (called junk or non-investment bonds).

Classification with respect to the maturity

Money market securities: Securities with original maturity of one year or less are called money market securities. US treasury bills, commercial papers issued by corporations are some examples of money market fixed income securities.

Capital market securities: Securities with original maturity of more than one year are called capital market securities. Fixed deposits and debentures are called capital market securities.

Classification with respect to coupon structure

Bonds are classified as fixed rate and floating rate according their coupon structure. Fixed rate bonds pays a certain amount periodically while floating rate bonds changes the coupon rate according to market rate of interest. Floating rate bonds are better in changing environment because when interest rate rises, the fixed bonds losses their value while floating rate bonds are adjusted accordingly.

Geography

Bonds can also be classified with respect to the issuance and trading geography. We have discussed it in very detail previously as domestic, global and Eurobonds.

Taxability

Some bonds are tax exempted (government and government related bonds are usually tax exempted) while others are taxed (as income tax and capital gain tax).

2: Describe types of fixed-income indexes

Companies, government and government agencies issue different types of fixed-income securities with different maturity, classes and preference of payment. So the universe of fixed-income securities and their indices is much wider than of shares. Fixed-income security indexes can be constructed on the basis of characteristics, geographical location, issuer etc.

Fixed-income securities are usually illiquid and sometimes index constructors need to contact dealers to obtain recent prices, which is a costly and time taking process.

3: Compare primary and secondary fixed-income markets to equity markets

Primary and secondary equity market:

The market in which the companies issue their securities for the first time is called primary market. **Primary market**

In primary market to types of transactions held

1. The newly issued stocks of a firm whose shares are not being traded in other market. This is called initial public offerings (IPOs).
2. The seasoned offering: The issuing of new stocks by a firm whose shares are being traded in secondary market.

The issuer get help from an investment banker to find the buyer for seasoned as well as IPos.

Investment banks provide two types of offerings for the sale of shares: underwritten offerings and best-effort offerings.

With an underwriting offering, the bank agrees to buy any unsold shares at a pre-negotiated price. Under the underwriting offering, the investment bank has a conflict of interest with the issuer. The issuer has hired the bank to sell its securities at higher prices, but the bank wants to reduce its own risk of buying unsold securities. Then, the bank wants to reduce the price and help the buyers buy the securities. Under best effort offering, the bank tries its best to sell the shares, but if any number of sales are unsold, the bank is not obliged to buy them.

The investment bank finds and attracts investors to buy the securities by issuing the issuer's financials. The investors who show interest will be evaluated and sold the shares. The public issue of financials and getting indication of interest is called book building or book runner. If indication of interest is greater than the number of shares to be offered the price can be adjusted upward and vice versa.

Secondary market

The subsequent issue or trade of securities between dealers and other market participants is held in secondary market.

Debt Market

Money market:
The market of debt securities with a maturity of one year or less.

Capital market:
The market in which debt or equity securities with maturity of longer than one year are being traded.

The primary debt market is the market in which the issuer issues the debt instruments for the first time (like IPOs in the equity market)

While the secondary debt market is used for the subsequent sale and purchase of debt instruments.

Comparison

The secondary debt market is usually less liquid than the secondary equity market.

A secondary equity market is usually the centralized exchange, while fixed-income securities are usually OTC.

LEARNING MODULE 4

Fixed-Income Markets for Corporate Issuers

1: Compare short-term funding alternatives available to corporations and financial institutions

Short-term funding alternatives for non-financial institutions

There are many types of financing sources available to a company. Each of these sources has its own benefits and risks. These sources can be divided into the following categories of internal financing and external financing.

Internal financing: Internal financing means using the company's own profits or assets to finance its projects. Following are some internal financing sources

    a. **Operating cash flows:** Cash flow received from operating activities minus taxes can be used to finance assets or other projects.
    b. **Account payables:** Deferring supplier payments can also be used to finance internally.
    c. **Account receivables:** Companies prefer to get early payment from customers. These receipts can be a source of internal financing.
    d. **Inventory:** The amount spent on inventory can be reallocated towards financing and productive use.
    e. **Marketable securities:** Instead of holding cash, companies invest in short-term securities, which can be easily converted into cash on demand. These securities can be converted to finance.

  External sources
    1. **Financing through Financial intermediaries:**

a. **Uncommitted line of credit**: A bank can provide an uncommitted line of credit to a company, but it's unreliable because the bank can refuse to finance at any time.
b. **Committed line of credit:** Also called regular line of credit, this is a short-term financing source. The bank comes under a commitment with the company to provide funds to finance its projects. It is a more reliable source than an uncommitted line of credit.
c. **Revolving credit arrangement or revolvers:** This is the most reliable source of financing than above two. Companies can draw funds from bank and pay back on periodic basis. It's also a short term financing source.
d. **Secured and un-secured loans:** Corporations can finance their projects or needs can borrow from the depository institutes. These funds are to be paid back in future. These loans can be available as secured or unsecured loans. The interest rate is high on unsecured loans. Companies may borrow to install new plant or to acquire other firms. The loans with collateral are called _secured loans_. There are some borrowings in which there is no collateral involved. These loans are called _unsecured loans_. The lender wants more interest rate as a premium as he is taking more risk.
e. **Web based lenders:** These are non-banking lenders which lend to usually small business who need cash to finance their operations and projects. These are usually short term.

2. **Capital market financing**
a. **Commercial papers:** Sound organizations can issue commercial papers for their short term funding needs (i.e. working capital) and bridge financing. Bridge financing means commercial papers can fulfill funding needs before the long term debt securities

Currency risk: It involve when a company raise capital in foreign market. If the company expect a favorable movement of exchange rate then it can raise capital from foreign market otherwise not.

Agency cost: If the company raise more and more debt the debt holders can protect themselves by using covenants. The company can use the cost benefit analysis on these covenants and choose the optimized combination of capital.

Bankruptcy: If a company is near bankruptcy, it has limited choices and even these choices are costly.

Floating costs: The costs related to issuance of debt or equity securities, legal fee or related expenses also impact the choice of financing.

Macroeconomic or general economic considerations

Tax, inflation, monetary and fiscal policies also affect the choice of financing.

Funding alternatives for the financial institutions

Retail market: Deposits by the customers in the banks (retail deposits) are the basic sources of funding for banks. With checking accounts (demand deposits) banks don't have to pay any interest payments and these funds are immediately available for bank's funding needs. With saving accounts banks has to pay some interest but client cannot withdraw them immediately.

Certificates of deposits (CDS): Banks also offer certificates of deposits for which the clients cannot withdraw the money before a maturity date if they do so they will have to pay a significant penalty. CDS are also good source of funding for the banks. The interest rate is higher in CDs.

Negotiable certificates of deposits: These are the short-term instruments issued by banks with the maturity ranging from 2 weeks to 1 year. These certificates can be sold at discount or they can give regular interest payments. The minimum face value must be $100000. Subsequently these certificates are traded in secondary market.

Interbank market: The banks can get funds from other banks on interbank rate usually at LIBOR rate. These funds can fulfill short-term need of the banks. These are the unsecured loans given by one bank to another with maturity of one day (overnight) to one year.

Central bank funds market: In US this is called FED fund market. The banks operating under central bank are required to deposit a certain amount with central banks. Sometimes some banks have excessive funds (from this reserve requirement) can lend excessive funds to other banks at central bank rate. These loans can mature from one day to one year. The interest rate depends on the central bank's monetary policy and open market operations.

2: Describe repurchase agreements (repos), their uses, and their benefits and risks

Repurchase agreement or REPO is an agreement in which one party sells a security to another party with agreement to buy it back at a specific (higher) price at later date. The difference between selling and buying back price is the interest payment by initial seller (borrower) of the security. The security severs as collateral and the interest rate is called repo rate. This repo rate is normally less than a bank loan. If this agreement is of one day it is called overnight repo and more than one day is called term repo.

Repo margin or haircut: The market value of that contract (bond) might be different from the amount of loan. The percentage difference between market value and amount of loan is called repo margin or haircut. For example if a security is sold for $100 and agreed to be repurchased back at $110 and the market value of that security is $105. The percentage difference between 105 and 100 is haircut. Haircut protects the lender from a decrease in value of underlying security.

Factors affecting repo rate and haircut:
The lender of funds is most vulnerable party in a repo agreement regardless of collateral. So the repo rate and haircut depends on following factors.

1. More the maturity more would be the repo rate and haircut and vice versa.
2. Higher the creditability of borrower and quality of security, lower the repo rate and haircut.
3. When collateral is delivered to lender the repo rate and haircut would be lower.
4. When market interest rate is higher the repo rate and haircut would be higher.
5. If the collateral has higher demand in market the repo rate and haircut would be lower.

Reverse repo agreement is agreement in which the lender of funds sells the security (opposite of buying the collateral as in normal repo).

3: Contrast the long-term funding of investment-grade versus high-yield corporate issuers

Investment grade bonds

Credit rating is provided by credit rating agencies like Standard and poor's (S&P), Moody's and Fitch. According to S&P and Fitch AAA, AA and BBB are investment grade bonds. According to Moody's Aaa to Baa3 are the investment grade bonds. The bonds rated below than these grades are high yielding yet riskier (called junk or non-investment bonds).

High yield debt

These are non-investment or junk bonds which are rated below Baa3/BBB. These bonds are rated lower because of following reasons.

1. High leverage

2. Issuing firm is in declining industry
3. Operating history is weak or unknown
4. Higher sensitivity to business cycle
5. Lack of or unclear competitive advantage
6. Low quality management
7. Very low or negative cash flows
8. Large off-balance sheet liabilities

As these bonds have higher default risk, special consideration must be taken in form of liquidity, financial projections, debt structure, corporate structure and covenants.

LEARNING MODULE 5

Fixed-Income Markets for Government Issuers

1: Describe funding choices by sovereign and non-sovereign governments, quasi-government entities, and supranational agencies

Sovereign governments

Bonds issued by the national governments for fiscal reasons are called sovereign bonds. These bonds are backed by taxing power and ability to print new money. That's why these bonds are considered default risk free bonds.

These bonds can be denominated in local or other currency. Bonds denominated in local currency are considered higher credit rated. This is because the government cannot print foreign currency and taxes are collected in local currency and its value in foreign currency depends on the exchange rate. US T-bills are good example of sovereign bond and these T-bills are used as benchmark for other bonds.

Sovereign bonds can be of fixed coupon rate, floating rate or inflation indexed bonds.

Non- Sovereign

Bonds issued by states, provinces, cities and regions and by entities created by state, or provinces to fund hospitals dams etc. are called non-sovereign government bonds. These bonds are not backed by national government but by the cash flows from specific projects for which bonds are issued (or can be backed by the cash flows from other projects). These bonds are normally traded at high yield. These bonds have high credit rating than other bonds but lower than the sovereign bonds.

Quasi-government or agency bonds: Bonds issued by specially created govt. agencies are quasi-government bonds. These bonds are issued for specific purpose. National government usually does not back these bonds but still these bonds are of high credit rating because the default risk is extremely low. Yield on these bonds is also high. In USA Federal National Mortgage Association is government created agency and its bonds are quasi-government bonds.

Supranational bonds: Bond issued by supranational agencies like World Bank and IMF are supranational bonds. These agencies are also called multilateral agencies. Credit rating of these bonds is also very high.

2: Contrast the issuance and trading of government and corporate fixed-income instruments

Issuance

When the bonds are issued first time they are issued in primary market. The first issuance can be to general public (public offering or initial public offering) or to selective investors called private placement. When bonds are initially sold, subsequently they are traded in secondary market.
Public offering is normally done through investment banks.
The investment banks can perform any of the following functions to assist sale of newly issued bonds.
Underwriting: Through underwriting services the investment banks purchases all the bonds from issuing entity and then resell them to the public or selected investors. Small number of bonds can be sold by a single bank but if the quantity of bonds is very large they are sold through syndicate of investment banks. The lead underwriter invites other banks to perform these duties.

Syndicate (or single bank in case of small offering) adjusts the price on which the bond would be sold.

Best effort offering: Through best effort offering the investment banks sells on commission basis. They earn commission on number of bonds sold and remaining will be returned to issuers.

Sometimes bonds are issued before public offer to check the demand for that bond. This is referred as *grey market.* Normally government and government related bonds like US treasury bills sold through auction are sold through best effort offering.

Shelf Registration: Through self-registration bonds are registered with security regulators in aggregate value. Then the bonds are issued overtime whenever the issuer needs funds. Shelf registration is normally allowed to sound and bigger companies. These issues can be sold through public offering or only to selective qualified investors.

Trading

When existing bonds (previously issued bonds) are traded that is called secondary market. The secondary market can be divided into two types an organized exchange and the over the counter market.

Organized exchange: This is the market where buyers and sellers trade securities with each other and the price is set through demand and supply. These buyers and sellers can be from anywhere in the world but they must follow the exchange rules. Exchange market provides higher liquidity. These bonds are cleared through clearing system. The settlement can be done at the day of trading, T+1, T+2 or T+3. T+1 mean settlement within trade day plus one day. The settlement can take even more than three days in some cases.

Over the counter market: In this market the trade is being done between parties without supervision of exchange. This is also called off-exchange-trading. In over the counter market there is less liquidity.

Difference between the issuance of government and corporate bonds

Corporate debt is often opportunistic and managed by investment banks. Government bonds are usually issued through public auctions and are managed by the Ministry of Finance. Corporate bonds are issued by posted-price selling.

Govt. bonds are usually OTC (with some exemptions) while corporate bonds are traded in centralized exchanges.

LEARNING MODULE 6

Fixed-Income Bond Valuation: Prices and Yields

1: Calculate a bond's price given a yield-to-maturity on or between coupon dates

2: Identify the relationships among a bond's price, coupon rate, maturity, and yield-to-maturity

The value of a bond is the present value of all future coupon and principal payments. This present value is calculated by using market discount rate also called yield to maturity or redemption yield.

Value of bond with annual coupon payment:

For example a 4-year-bond with face value of $100, coupon rate is 5% annually and market discount rate is 5% calculate present value of bond or simply value of bond.

Value of bond = $\frac{5}{1.05^1} + \frac{5}{1.05^2} + \frac{5}{1.05^3} + \frac{105}{1.05^4} = 100$

The present value of this bond is $100. Note that when the coupon rate and discount rate are same the present value of all future payments is equal to the par value.

For calculator input values are as follows;

N (number of years) =4, PMT (coupon payment) =5, FV=100, 1/Y (discount rate) =5.

If the discount rate is more than coupon rate the bond would be sold at discount. For example if discount rate is 10% the value of same bond would be

Value of bond = $\dfrac{5}{1.1^1} + \dfrac{5}{1.1^2} + \dfrac{5}{1.1^3} + \dfrac{105}{1.1^4}$ = 84.15 this is called discounted bond

So when the bond yield increases the present value and market value of bond decreases.

And when market yield (discount rate) decreases, the present value (or the market value) of bond increases called premium bond.

Value of bond with semi-annual coupon payment: Consider the same bond with 10% annual coupon rate semi-annually. The discount rate is also 10%. We need to convert 10% annual coupon rate in semi-annual as 10/2=5% of face value. Now the discounting periods are doubled (twice every year) so we have 4x2 = 8 periods of payment. The discount rate would also be divided by 2 as 10/2=5%.

Value of bond = $\dfrac{5}{1.05^1} + \dfrac{5}{1.05^2} + \dfrac{5}{1.05^3} + \dfrac{5}{1.05^4} + \dfrac{5}{1.05^5} + \dfrac{5}{1.05^6} + \dfrac{5}{1.05^7} + \dfrac{105}{1.05^8}$ = 100

If price of bond, number of years and coupon rates are given we can also calculate yield to maturity. The YTM would be the rate which makes the present value of future cash flow equal to the price of bond.

- As we have discussed in previous L O S the discount rate (yield to maturity) rate is inversely related to the market value of bond. When discount rate increases (decreases) the price of bond decreases (increases). When discount rate (YTM) and coupon rate is equal the bond is at par. When YTM is greater than coupon rate the bond is at discount and when YTM is less than coupon rate the bond is at premium.
- When YTM increases the percentage decrease in value of bond is smaller than the increase in bond's value as YTM decreases with same amount. So the price to yield relationship is convex.
- The bond with lower coupon rate is more sensitive to a change in YTM than a bond with higher coupon rate.

- The bond with higher maturity term is more sensitive to change in YTM than a bond with lower maturity. This is because when a bond's maturity is longer it will be discounted more times.

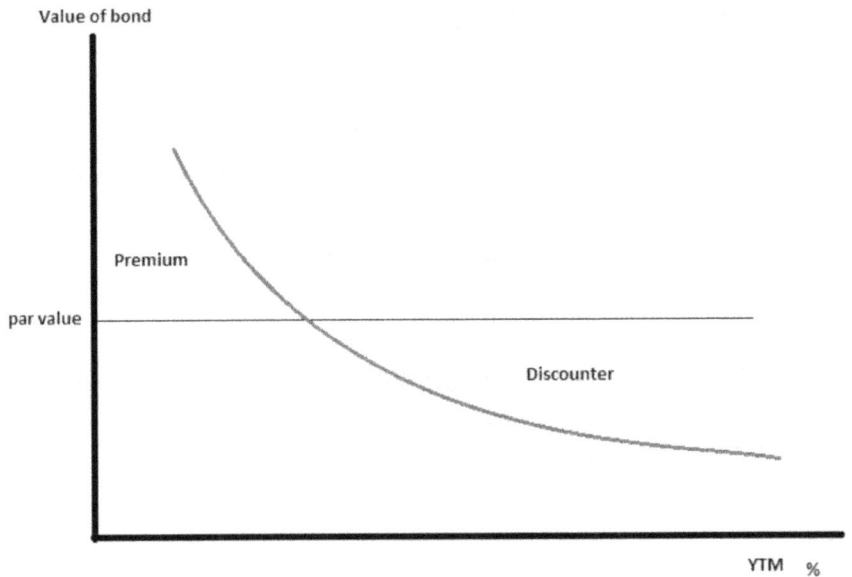

Before maturity the bond can traded at par, discount or at premium. Regardless of the current value of bond the price will converge to the par as the maturity approaches. This convergence is called constant-yield price trajectory.

The price of bond differs in between coupon payments. This price has two components: the flat price (PV_{flat}) and accrued interest (AI). The full price (PV_{full}) is the sum of AI and flat price. This full price is also called dirty price. $PV_{flat} + AI = PV_{full}$

The flat value can be calculated on a specific date is simply the present value of remaining coupons and principal amount.

Accrued interest can be calculated as

$AI = (t/T) \times PMT$

T is the number of days passed from last coupon payment.
T = Total number of days between two payments.

3: Describe matrix pricing

The method of estimation of price of a bond which is not being actively traded (or not being traded) is called matrix pricing. This estimation is used to calculate price and YTM of infrequently traded bonds. We use the prices of the other most actively traded bonds with similar credit quality, maturity date and coupon rate in estimation.

For example we have illiquid bond A with coupon rate of 5% and maturity of 3 years.
We also found two related bonds with active market as follows;
Bond Y with 4years of maturity and coupon rate of 5.5% at price of 102.
Bond Z with 2 years of maturity and coupon rate of 4.5% at price of 101.
The YTM on bond Y can be calculated as
With bond Y we have
N=4, PV=-102, PMT=5.5, FV=100, calculate 1/y
With bond Z we have
N=2, PV=-101, PMT=4.5, FV=100, calculate 1/y
When we will have YTM on these two bonds we can take average of YTMs of two bonds and use it as estimated YTM on our bond A. from here we can calculate the price of our bond using this average YTM.

Matrix pricing can also be used in underwriting process to get an estimation of YTM and spread over benchmark (mostly a similar government bond).

LEARNING MODULE 7

Yield and Yield Spread Measures for Fixed-Rate Bonds

1: Calculate annual yield on a bond for varying compounding periods in a year

Annual yield = $\{1+(i/n)\}^{\wedge}n)-1$

"n" is number of compounding annually.

"i" is nominal yield

For example annual paying 4% YTM bond has annual yield (also called effective yield) of 4%.

Annual yield = $[\{1+(i/n)\}^{\wedge}2]-1 = [\{1+(0.004/1)\}^{\wedge}1] - 1 = 4\%$.

Semiannual bond with 4% nominal yield has annual yield of $((1+0.04/2)^{\wedge}2\} - 1 = 4.04\%$.

Same way we can calculate annual yields for quarterly, monthly or of any periodicity.

2: Compare, calculate, and interpret yield and yield spread measures for fixed-rate bonds

Yield spread: Difference between yields of two different bonds is called yield spread.
This spread is usually calculated with respect to a benchmark called _benchmark spread._ For example a 2-year corporate bond yield is 5% and 2-yeargovernment bond yield is 3% the yield

spread of corporate bond is 5-3= 2%. This yield spread is usually calculated in basis points. We know that 1% is equal to 100 basis points. So yield spread in our case is 200 basis points. Yield spread with respect to government security is also called _G-spread_.

The yield spread must be calculated by comparing two securities of same maturities. Yield spread can also change during life of the bond. For example when a 4-year bond is issued it is compared with 5-year security and after 1 year passes its spread can be compared with a security with maturity of 4 years.

Yield spread can also be calculated with respect to a swap (with same currency). This is known as _interpolated spread (I-spread)._

For analysis if the yield on a specific security rises but spread remains same it means overall yields have risen due to economic growth (or any other macroeconomic variable). On the other hand if the spread has risen the credit risk of issuer may be increased.

Z-spread or zero volatility spread: The yield on bonds increases with maturity. The simple spread will increase as the maturity of bond increases. So the simple yield spreads (I-spread and G-spread) have this disadvantage because they shows higher yield with higher maturity.

Eliminate this problem we have Z-spread. To calculate Z-spread we have to add some appropriate amount in the benchmark so the new benchmark yield equalizes the price of bond to its market value. This is how we calculate z-spread;

$$\text{Market price of bond} = \frac{\text{coupon PMT}}{\text{benchmarke} + Z} + \frac{\text{coupon PMT}}{\text{benchmarke} + Z} + \frac{\text{coupon PMT}}{\text{benchmarke} + Z} \cdots \frac{\text{coupon PMTn}}{\text{benchmarke} + Z}$$

If we are given market price, coupon payment and bench mark we can calculate the Z-spread with the help of this equation by trial and error basis. Remember that Z must be constant across all periods.

The Z-spread tend to be higher (lower) with more (less) credit risk.

Option adjusted spread: The option adjusted spread is calculated for the bonds with options of call or put. Simple spread or z- spread cannot accurately calculate yield on callable/put-able bond.

We know that the price of a callable bond is less than equivalent non-callable bond. So we calculate the option adjusted spread by removing the option on that bond.

Option embedded spread = Z-spread − option value

Yield Measures for Fixed-rate bonds

Yield to maturity: The YTM depends on the number of coupon payment in a year.

Effective yield: Effective yield is measure of return assuming that the amount received (coupon payment) is reinvested at same interest rate.

Effective yield = $\{1+(YTM/n)\}^{\wedge}n)-1$

"n" is number of compounding annually.

For example annual paying 4% YTM bond has effective yield of 4%. Semiannual bond with 4% annual YTM has yield of 4/2 = 2% every six months and effective yield is $((1+0.04/2)^{\wedge}2) - 1$ = 4.04%.

Effective yield is used to convert the YTM in a comparable mode.

Current yield: It is calculated by sing annual coupon payments and bond's price

Current yield = $\frac{\text{Annual coupon payment}}{\text{Current market price of bond}}$

This measure is very simple and does not count the capital gain/loss and does not give us any other information.

Street conversion: Street conversion assumes that the coupon payments are made on actual date (on Saturdays and Sundays if stated so).

True yield: True yield is calculated by taking the dates on which the coupon payments are made. If the stated payment date is on weekends they are actually paid in next working days. So the true yields are slightly lower than street conversion.

Yield to worst: This measure is used to calculate yield in worst case scenario to help the investor to manage risk. This is the lowest potential yield that investor would receive without issuer actually defaulted.

Yield to call: It is calculated for each call date of a security.

Yields on Floating rate Notes (FRNs)

The return on floating rate notes is adjusted periodically according to the reference (Usually LIBOR) plus/minus a margin. Due to flexibility of interest rate (rate of return) the price of FRNs is generally more stable. This margin depends on the credit risk of issuer. The rate quoted on FRNs is called *quoted margin* and the margin to make its present value equal to it par value is called *required margin*. If credit risk of issuer increases (decreases) over the tem of FRN, the quoted margin would be lower (higher) than required margin and the FRN will be sold at discount (premium). With no change in credit risk these two would be equal at each reset point and the price would be at par.

Rule for calculation is same here. At each reset date the current reference rate is used to calculate future cash flow and discount it at required rate.

LEARNING MODULE 8

Yield and Yield Spread Measures for Floating-Rate Instruments

1: Calculate and interpret yield spread measures for floating-rate instruments

Yields on Floating rate instruments

The return on floating rate instruments is adjusted periodically according to the reference (Usually LIBOR) plus/minus a margin. Due to flexibility of interest rate (rate of return) the price of FRNs is generally more stable. This margin depends on the credit risk of issuer. The rate quoted on FRNs is called *quoted margin* and the margin to make its present value equal to it par value is called *required margin*. If credit risk of issuer increases (decreases) over the tem of FRN, the quoted margin would be lower (higher) than required margin and the FRN will be sold at discount (premium). With no change in credit risk these two would be equal at each reset point and the price would be at par.

Rule for calculation is same here. At each reset date the current reference rate is used to calculate future cash flow and discount it at required rate.

2: Calculate and interpret yield measures for money market instruments

Yields for Money Market Instruments

The yield on money market instruments is calculated as discount from face value or add-on yield using 360 or 365 days. US T-bills are quoted as annual discount rate using 360 days. The CDs are quoted with add-on rate using 365 days. So the difference between discount rate and add-on rate is only the total days in calculation.

Formulae

$$\text{Discount rate} = \frac{\text{days in a year}}{\text{number of days in maturity of intrument}} * \frac{FV - PV}{PV}$$

$$\text{ADD on rate} = \frac{\text{days in a year}}{\text{number of days in maturity of intrument}} * \frac{FV - PV}{PV}$$

LEARNING MODULE 9

The Term Structure of Interest Rates: Spot, Par, and Forward Curves

1: Define spot rates and the spot curve, and calculate the price of a bond using spot rates

Spot rates are the yield to maturity (discount rate) on zero coupon bonds maturing at each cash flow date. Yield to maturity is calculated as the discount rate is same for every bond. But actually discount rate depends on the timing of each cash flow that's why spot rate is more relevant for discounting a bond. This discount rate on zero coupon bonds is also called zero coupon rates or zero rates. To calculate bond's price using spot rate we discount each cash flow by its own spot rate and sum all the results as follows;

Value of bond = $\frac{CF1}{1.S1^1} + \frac{CF2}{(1.S2)^2} + \frac{CF3}{(1.S3)^3} + \frac{CF4}{(1.S4)^4} + \frac{CF5}{1.S5^5} \ldots \ldots \frac{CFn}{(1.Sj)^n}$

CF1 = first cash flow on that bond
CF2 = second cash flow on that bond
CFn = Final cash flow of bond. It consisted of coupon plus principal amount.
S1 = the spot rate at time of first cash flow
S2 = spot rate at time of second cash flow
Sn = spot rate at time of maturity.

For example we have 3-year bond with FV of $100 and coupon rate is 5%. Spot rates are
1-year sport rate = 2%
2-year spot rate = 4%
5-year spot rate 5%.

Then value of bond = $\frac{5}{1.02^1} + \frac{5}{(1.04)^2} + \frac{105}{(1.05)^3}$ = 100.22

As the price of bond is greater than its FV the YTM would be less than its coupon rate.

By using calculator we can calculate YTM by inputting following data.

N=3, PMT=5, FV=100, PV= 100.22 calculate 1/y

The bond price using spot rate is also called no arbitrage price. So when the price is different from 100.22 in our case there would be a profitable opportunity.

Spot rate curve: YTM on zero coupon bonds is called spot rates. Curve representing this relationship between YTM on zero coupon bond and maturity of bond is called spot rate curve, strip curve or zero curve.

US treasury bonds are considered as zero coupon bonds. Higher the maturity more the YTM is.

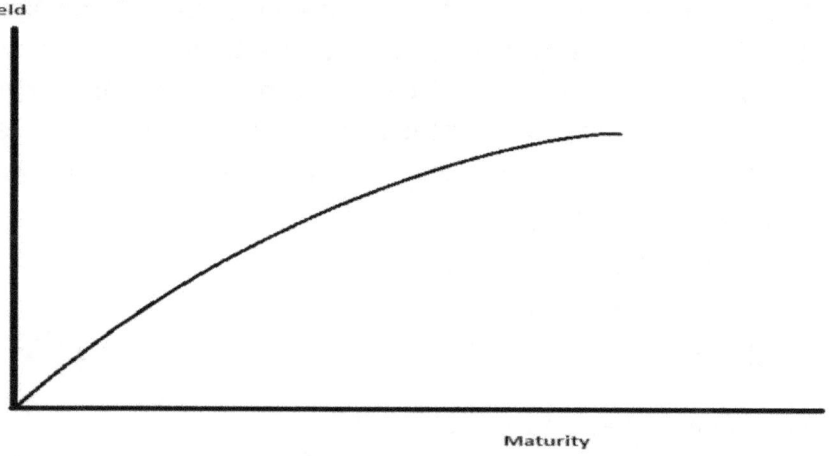

2: Define par and forward rates, and calculate par rates, forward rates from spot rates, spot rates from forward rates, and the price of a bond using forward rates

Forward rate is the interest rate on a loan beginning at some future date. Spot rate is the interest rate on a loan beginning immediately. Forward rate for 1y2y means forward rate from one year from now for two year loan. First notion (1y) states future date and second notion (2y) states the term of loan.

Relationship between forward rates and spot rates

Logically borrowing for 4 years at 4-year spot rate and borrowing for one year for 4 consecutive years must be at same cost. This logic can be expressed in following equation.

$$(1 + S4)^4 = (1 + S1)(1 + 1y1y)(1 + 2y1y)(1 + 3y1y)$$

Left hand side shows the four spot rates for 4 consecutive years while right hand side shows forward rates. First term (1+S1) states that in first year it is the current rate which would be used. Ok solve the previous equation for S4

$$S4 = \{(1 + S1)(1 + 1y1y)(1 + 2y1y)(1 + 3y1y)\}^{1/4} - 1$$

This term on right hand side is simply the geometric mean of three terms.

This very same relationship can be used to calculate forward rate with given spot rate.

Calculation of bond's value using forward rates:

This is also very simple calculation. Just discount every cash payment of bond by forward rate for each period.

$$\text{Bond value using forward rate} = \frac{PMT1}{1+S1} + \frac{PMT2}{(1+S1)(1+1y1y)} + \frac{PMT3}{(1+S1)(1+1y1y)(1+2y1y)} \cdots \frac{PMTn}{(1+S1)(1+1y1y)((1+ny1y)}$$

A par rate (par yield) is the yield for which bond is priced at par. Consider a 4-year annual coupon bond and spot rates are as follows;

1-year spot rate is S1=2%

2-year spot rate is S2=1.8%

3-year spot rate is S3 = 2.1%

4-year spot rate is S4 = 2.2%

We can calculate par bond yield as

$$\frac{PMT}{(1+S1)^1} + \frac{PMT}{(1+S2)^2} + \frac{PMT}{(1+S3)^3} + \frac{100+PMT}{(1+S4)^4}$$

$$\frac{PMT}{(1+0.02)^1} + \frac{PMT}{(1+0.018)^2} + \frac{PMT}{(1+0.021)^3} + \frac{100+PMT}{(1+0.022)^4}$$

Solving for PMT we will have par bond yield.

3: Compare the spot curve, par curve, and forward curve

Spot rate curve: YTM on zero coupon bonds is called spot rates. Curve representing this relationship between YTM on zero coupon bond and maturity of bond is called spot rate curve, strip curve or zero curve.

US treasury bonds are considered as zero coupon bonds. Higher the maturity more the YTM is.

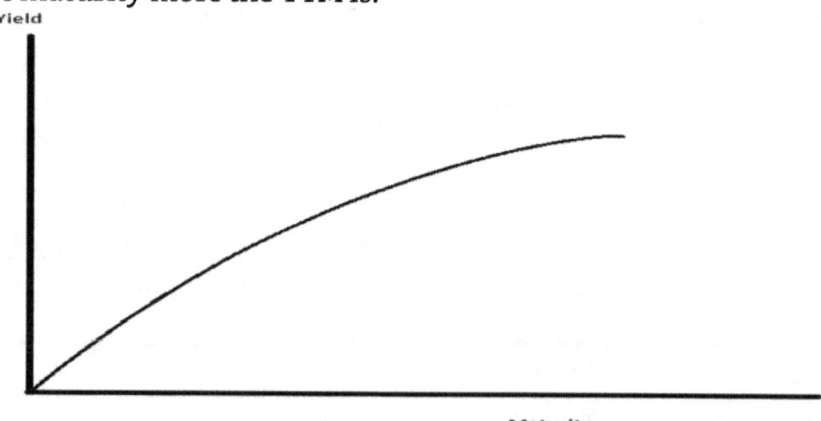

Par bond yield curve: Also called par curve. It is not constructed from the actual cash payments but from spot rate curve. A par yield is the yield for which bond is priced at par. Consider a 4-year annual coupon bond and spot rates are as follows;
1-year spot rate is S1=2%
2-year spot rate is S2=1.8%
3-year spot rate is S3=2.1%
4-year spot rate is S4=2.2%
We can calculate par bond yield as

$$\frac{PMT}{(1+S1)^1} + \frac{PMT}{(1+S2)^2} + \frac{PMT}{(1+S3)^3} + \frac{100+PMT}{(1+S4)^4}$$

$$\frac{PMT}{(1+0.02)^1} + \frac{PMT}{(1+0.018)^2} + \frac{PMT}{(1+0.021)^3} + \frac{100+PMT}{(1+0.022)^4}$$

Solving for PMT we will have par bond yield.

Yield curve for coupon bonds: Curve shows relationship between yield and maturity of coupon bonds. Again higher maturities have higher yield.

LEARNING MODULE 10

Interest Rate Risk and Return

1: Calculate and interpret the sources of return from investing in a fixed-rate bond

By assuming that the coupon and principal amount is paid on time and the coupon received can be reinvested at same YTM, there are four sources of return from fixed rate bond

1. Coupon amount
2. Principal amount
3. Interest earned on reinvestment of coupon payments
4. Capital gain from prematurity sale.

When an investor buys and holds a fixed rate bond until maturity then the investor earns annualized rate of return equal to YTM at purchase.

If an investor sales the bond before maturity he will earn rate of return equal to YTM at purchase if the YTM of that bond does not change.

If market rate of return (YTM) increases after the purchase of bond the investor can reinvest at higher rate so YTM increases and it would be higher than the YTM at purchase.

If market rate of return (YTM) decreases after the purchase of bond the investor can reinvest at lower rate so YTM decreases and it would be lower than the YTM at purchase.

2: Describe the relationships among a bond's holding period return, its Macaulay duration, and the investment horizon

3: Define, calculate, and interpret Macaulay duration.

CFA LEVEL1 FIXED INCOME

$$\text{Holding Period Return} = \frac{\text{Coupon payments} + (\text{End of Period Value} - \text{Initial Value})}{\text{Initial Value}}$$

Macaulay duration: It is the weighted average term to maturity of cash flows from fixed income bond. This was first introduced by Frederick Macaulay. It is actually the measure of bond's price sensitivity to change in interest rate. It shows how many numbers of years a bond should be held by investor until the present value of bond's cash flows equals the price paid for the bond.

$$\text{Macaulay duration} = \sum_{t=1}^{n} \frac{tC}{(1+\text{YTM})^t} + \frac{nV}{(1+\text{YTM})^n} \div MP$$

t= period in which coupon is received
n= total number of periods
C=Coupon payments
YTM is yield to maturity or required yield
V=Maturity value
MP= Market price of bond

The above formula seems complex but actually the calculation is very simple as follows; the present value of cash flows weighted by the duration of each cash flow divided by current market price. Consider a 3-year $100 bond with annual coupon rate of 10%.

Period	Cash flow	Cash flow x period	Present value of each cash flow
1	10	10	9.09091
2	10	20	16.53
3	110	330	247.93
Total			273.551

Macaulay duration = 273.551/100 = 2.73
Now this bond has sensitivity of 2.73. If the interest rate changes by 30 basis points Macaulay duration would change by 2.73 x 0.0030 = 0.00819 duration.

Investment horizon plays an important role in decision making

41

for investors. A short term change in interest rate is of great concern for investor who needs to sale bond before maturity. Investor with long term horizon is less concerned with short term interest rate changes because these changes creates unrealized gains/losses but this investor is looking for total return over investment horizon.

If interest rate rises (falls) the by-and- hold investor has higher (lower) total gain. This is because with rise in interest rate the price of bond falls (according to duration measures) but at maturity the price will be pulled to par. The gain on reinvestments of coupon payments is greater now (because market rate is higher). Opposite to this happens when interest rate falls.

The relationship among holding period return, duration and investment horizon can be described in following way.

When investment horizon is greater than Macaulay duration and interest rate falls the reinvestment of coupons will give less return. The increase in price of bond due to fall in interest rate is less important as the investment horizon is longer and short term volatility is not of greater concern. When investment horizon is greater than Macaulay duration and interest rate increases, the investor will gain from reinvestment of coupons. The reduction in price of bond due to increase in interest rate will be less as the holding period is longer.

Opposite to this happens when investment horizon is less than Macaulay duration.

When investment horizon and Macaulay duration are equal, any fall or rise in interest rate will make the price of bond and total return to offset each other.

The difference between Macaulay duration and investment horizon is called duration gap.
Duration gap = Macaulay duration - investment horizon
Duration gap changes with the passage of time as investment horizon and Macaulay duration changes.

LEARNING MODULE 11

Yield-Based Bond Duration Measures and Properties

1: Define, calculate, and interpret modified duration, money duration, and the price value of a basis point (PVBP)

Consider a 3-year $100 bond with annual coupon rate of 10%.

Period	Cash flow	Cash flow x period	Present value of each cash flow
1	10	10	9.09091
2	10	20	16.53
3	110	330	247.93
Total			273.551

Macaulay duration = 273.551/100 = 2.73
Now this bond has sensitivity of 2.73. If the interest rate changes by 30 basis points Macaulay duration would change by 2.73 x 0.0030 = 0.00819 duration.

Modified duration: It shows percentage change in price of bond due to percentage change in yield to maturity.
Modified duration = Macaulay duration/ (1+YTM/q)
Where q is the number of times a bond pays in one year. For annual bond q is 1 and for semi-annual bond q is 2.
Using previous case
Modified duration (ModDur) = 2.73/1.1 = 2.48
2.48 shows if YTM increases by 1 percent the price of bond will fall by 2.48 percent.

Money Duration: We know that modified duration measures the percentage change in price of a bond due to percentage change in yield to maturity.

Money duration (in US called dollar duration) measures the change in bond price in absolute terms (in currency).

Money duration = full price + Annual modified duration

Δ full price $\cong$ – MoneyDur x ΔYield

Money duration is also expressed as money duration per 100 of bond par value.

Money duration per 100 units of par value = annual modified duration × full bond price per 100 of par value

Price value of a basis point (PVBP): It is the money change in the full price of a bond due to change in its YTM by 1 basis point.

PVBP = Δ full price/ Δ YTM

2: Explain how a bond's maturity, coupon, and yield level affect its interest rate risk

Maturity and interest rate risk: Other things remains same bond with longer maturity is more sensitive to interest rate change. This is because the more a coupon payment would be made in future the more it will be discounted. So the shorter period bond has less interest rate risk.

Coupon rate and interest rate risk: By holding other thing constant bond with higher (lower) coupon payments has lower (higher) interest rate risk.

Yield and interest rate: Higher (lower) the yield lower (higher) the interest rate risk.

LEARNING MODULE 12

Yield-Based Bond Convexity and Portfolio Properties

1: Calculate and interpret convexity and describe the convexity adjustment

We know that modified duration is the linear approximation of changes in yield and price. But the actual relationship between yield and price is not linear but convex. Due to the convex relationship the modDur approximation does not give us good results with as the yield curve becomes more and more convex. The convexity here means when the yield increases the price of bond fall but at decreasing rate. It also means convexity saves the bond older from sudden decrease in price when yield changes.

Convexity: It is a measure of the yield curve in relation to price. It is used to measure non-linear relationships.

$$\text{Approximate Convexity} = \frac{\{P(i\ decreased) + P(i\ increased) - 2P0\}}{P0(\Delta YTM)^2}$$

P(i decrease) means price of bond when interest rate falls.
P(i increase) means price of bond when interest rate increases.
P0 is the initial price which is face value.

When there are embedded options with the bond we use effective convexity.

$$\text{Approximate effective convexity} = \frac{\{P(i\ decreased) + P(i\ increased) - 2P0\}}{P0(\Delta curve)^2}$$

Bonds with embedded options have more convexity than option free similar bonds. Longer maturity bonds, lower coupon rate and lower YTM are also exposed to more convexity.

Convexity adjustment:

Multiplying the change in the yield-to-maturity squared by half of the annual convexity statistic (AnnConvexity) is the convexity adjustment. The modified estimate gets rather close to the real price on the curved line after adding this amount to the linear estimate given by the time alone. We use the symbol "≈" as the final adjusted price is just a rough approximation.

2: Calculate the percentage price change of a bond for a specified change in yield, given the bond's duration and convexity

Change in full price of bond = - Annual ModDur x ΔYTM + { ½ x annual convexity x (ΔYTM^2)}

3: Calculate portfolio duration and convexity and explain the limitations of these measures

There are two methods to calculate duration of portfolio;
        1. Weighted average period until receipts cash flows
        2. Weighted average duration of each bond in portfolio

The first method is theoretically better but very hard to implement. Second method is easy to implement but has more limitations.

Weighted average period until receipts cash flows:

The first method is based on the cash flow yield (IRR). The calculation is as follows;

Total value of portfolio = $\dfrac{\text{Cash flow1}}{(1+r)^1} + \dfrac{\text{Cash flow2}}{(1+r)^2} + \ldots\ldots \dfrac{\text{Cash flow n}}{(1+r)^n}$

And calculate for r.

<u>Limitations:</u> This method cannot be used when future cash flows are uncertain. Future cash flows are uncertain in case of bonds with embedded options or floating rate bonds. Secondly interest rate risk (changes) is not usually expressed as spread to benchmark. Thirdly the yield is not calculated for bond portfolios.

Moreover this method is hard to implement.

Weighted average duration of each bond in portfolio:
In this method we calculate the weighted average duration of individual bonds and add them.

Portfolio duration = W1 D1 + W2 D2 + ... + Wn Dn

W1 is the weight of first bond which is calculated as full price of that bond divided by total value of the portfolio.
W2 is the weight of second bond and so on.
D1 is the duration of first bond, D2 is the duration of second bond and so on.
N is the number of bonds in portfolio.

Limitations: This method is useful even in case of bonds with embedded options (by taking effective duration). This approach is less accurate than first one but it is easy to implement.
Another limitation of this approach is the change in yield of each bond must be same otherwise this measure will not make good sense.

LEARNING MODULE 13

Curve-Based and Empirical Fixed-Income Risk Measures

1: Explain why effective duration and effective convexity are the most appropriate measures of interest rate risk for bonds with embedded options

Macaulay duration: It is the weighted average term to maturity of cash flows from fixed income bond.

$$\text{Macaulay duration} = \sum_{t=1}^{n} \frac{tC}{(1+\text{YTM})^t} + \frac{nV}{(1+\text{YTM})^n} \div MP$$

Modified duration: It shows percentage change in price of bond due to percentage change in yield to maturity.
Modified duration = Macaulay duration/ (1+YTM/q)

Effective duration: With above two discussed methods we assumed option free security (no call or put option and no prepayments). These embedded options change the bond's yield. With effective duration we take these embedded options into account to calculate bond's price.

$$\text{Effective duration} = \frac{P_- - P_+}{((2*P0)*(Y_- - Y_+))}$$

P_- is the price of bond if yield falls by x basis points.
P_+ is the price of bond if yield rises by x basis points.
Po is the initial price of bond.

$Y_- - Y_+$ is the changes in yield.

2: Calculate the percentage price change of a bond for a specified change in benchmark yield, given the bond's effective duration and convexity

Change in full price of bond = - Annual ModDur x ΔYTM + { ½ x annual convexity x (ΔYTM^2)}

3: Define key rate duration and describe its use to measure price sensitivity of fixed-income instruments to benchmark yield curve changes

The duration measures are only useful when there is no change in the shape of benchmark yield (the shift was parallel). When the yield curve changes its shape (become steeper or flatter) the key rate duration (also called partial duration) helps us to measure the sensitivity of bond's (or portfolio's) price of a specific maturity towards changes in benchmark yield. In case of portfolio we measure the key rate duration for each maturity and total effect is the sum of these individual results.

4: Describe the difference between empirical duration and analytical duration

Analytical duration and empirical duration both are used to measure bond`s price sensitivity to the interest rate change.

Analytical duration is calculated based on the premise that the government bond yield and spreads are independent of one another. Analytical duration examines the impact of changes in benchmark yields on bond prices.

The term "**empirical duration**" describes the process of building statistical models to estimate duration from past data. A wide range of variables influencing bond prices are included in the statistical data. Empirical duration is considered more accurate and mostly used for the decision-making process.

LEARNING MODULE 14

Credit Risk

1: Describe credit risk and its components, probability of default and loss given default

Credit risk: It is a risk that the borrower will fail to pay back the required payments (interest and principal amount).
Credit risk contains two elements;
Default risk/Default probability: The probability that the borrower will fail to pay the principal and interest payments at due date.
Loss severity: It is the risk from investor of bond that the issuer will default.
Credit related risks
Expected loss = default risk x loss severity
Recovery rate = value of security when issuer defaults. It can also be stated as percentage of a bond that investor will receive if issuer defaults.
Spread risk: It is the risk that the spread will change due to change in liquidity of bond and or due to change in creditworthiness of issuer. When bond's liquidity falls the spread increases and when issuer's creditworthiness falls the spread increases.
Credit migration or downgrade risk: The risk that the creditworthiness will fall.
Market liquidity risk: The risk that the liquidity of bond will fall.

2: Describe the uses of ratings from credit rating agencies and their limitations

Credit rating agencies like Moody's and Standard & Poor's and Fitch rate the bonds according to their default risk of the issuer. The bonds with same credit risk are assigned similar ratings. These agencies not only rate the corporations who issues these bonds but also rate the issue (the bond). The issuer's rating depends upon the creditworthiness. Senior unsecured bonds are used in rating process. Issuer's rating is called corporate family rating (CFR) and issue rating is called corporate credit rating (CCR). When one bond is considered as defaulted, this can trigger the default risk of the other bonds issued by same issuer. This is called default cross provision.

Following are the ratings assigned by the most popular three rating agencies.

Investment rating		Non-investment rating	
S&P, Fitch	Moody's	S&P, Fitch	Moody's
AAA	Aaa	BB+	Ba1
AA+	Aa1	BB	Ba2
AA	Aa2	BB-	Ba3
AA-	Aa3	B+	B1
A+	A1	B	B2
A	A2	B-	B3
A-	A3	CCC+	Caa1
BBB+	Baa1	CCC	Caa2
BBB	Baa2	CCC-	Caa3
BBB-	Baa3	CC	Ca
		C	C
		D	

According to S&P and Fitch the highest grade is AAA while with Moody's the highest grade is Aaa. The bonds from AAA (or Aaaa) to BBB- (or Baa3) are considered investment bonds. The bonds from BB+ (or Ba1) and lower are considered non-investment/ high yield/ low grade/junk bonds.

The bond issuer can issue bonds with respect to different maturities, different coupon rates and also with different credit ratings. The process of assigning different credit rating to the bonds issued by same corporation (or any other issuer) is called "nothing". Nothing can be based on covenants, seniority of bond and the risk of default.

For example a parent company issues a bond and the subsidiary company also issues a bond. If the subsidiary company's bond has a provision that it cannot send the funds to parent company unless the debt obligations are met. This can make the bonds of subsidiary company more credible than parent company.

Limitations

We can rely on the ratings issued by credible rating agencies but these ratings also have limitations;

Ratings tend to lag the market price: The market price move up and down more quickly than then rating agencies changes their rating.

Rating agencies can make mistakes: Although it does not usually happen but the rating agencies are not perfect. They may rate a security lower or higher by mistake.

Credit rating changes over the term of a security: Rating agencies adjust the rating time to time. Usually higher the rating is the more it would be stable.

Some risks are hard to calculate: Some risks cannot be calculated. For example litigation risk on certain commodities like tobacco and alcohol cannot be completely estimated. On the other hand natural calamities like earthquakes are hard to predict.

3: Describe macroeconomic, market, and issuer-specific factors that influence the level and volatility of yield spreads

We know that

Yield on a corporate bond = Real risk free interest rate + Expected inflation rate + Maturity premium + Liquidity premium + Credit spread

And
Yield spread = Liquidity premium + Credit spread
Spread yield can be influenced by following factors;

1. **Credit cycle:** As credit cycle improves (deteriorated) the spread gets narrow (widen) because it is perceived less (more) credit risk.
2. **Economic conditions:** With better economic conditions market perceived risk is lower so the spread narrows and vice versa.
3. **Overall financial market performance:** When the financial market is more efficient and performs well and is less volatile, the credit spread gets lower.
4. **Broker/dealer's willingness:** Yield spread narrows when the brokers are willing to provide sufficient funds for bond market to function.
5. **Market demand and supply:** In times of high demand the yield spread gets narrow. In case of more supply of bonds the spread widens.

LEARNING MODULE 15

Credit Analysis for Government Issuers

1: Explain special considerations when evaluating the credit of sovereign and non-sovereign government debt issuers and issues

High yield debt

These are non-investment or junk bonds which are rated below Baa3/BBB. These bonds are rated lower because of following reasons.

        9. High leverage
- 10. Issuing firm is in declining industry
- 11. Operating history is weak or unknown
- 12. Higher sensitivity to business cycle
- 13. Lack of or unclear competitive advantage
- 14. Low quality management
- 15. Very low or negative cash flows
- 16. Large off-balance sheet liabilities

As these bonds have higher default risk, special consideration must be taken in form of liquidity, financial projections, debt structure, corporate structure and covenants.

Sovereign debt

Sovereign bonds are issued by national governments. The bonds issued by developed country's government are considered to be risk free bonds. The analyst in case of these bonds must focus on the government's ability to pay and willingness to pay its debts. To assess the sovereign bonds following factors must be considered;

        1. Institutional effectiveness: It is the ability

of government in decision making and its implementation and also the rate of corruption in the institutes.
2. Economic growth prospects: The rate of growth in per-capita income, resource mobilization and stability and related issues.
3. International position: Foreign reserves, foreign investment, external debt and stability of exchange rate.
4. Flexibility in fiscal and monetary policy: The government's ability to generate cash flows by increasing taxes or to cut down expenditures. On the other hand central bank's ability to change monetary policy.

Non-sovereign government's bonds

These bonds are issued by government entities. These entities have not any ability to change the monetary or fiscal policies.

LEARNING MODULE 16

Credit Analysis for Corporate Issuers

1: Describe the qualitative and quantitative factors used to evaluate a corporate borrower's creditworthiness

Credit analysis is used to analyze the borrower`s ability to repay the debt. That analysis is also called credit worthiness. There are several factors which affect the creditworthiness of corporate borrower.

A. Qualitative factors

Corporate governance

1. Use of funds: The corporations should clearly tell what they are going to do with the borrowed money
2. Legal, tax, accounting: The rules are being followed by the borrower affect the credit worthiness. The corporation who is following proper accounting and tax regulations have higher creditworthiness.
3. Covenants: These are the restrictions imposed on issuer (borrower). These usually include restrictions on sale or pledging of same collateral asset and restrictions on additional borrowings. These covenants protect the bond holder's interests and reduce the default risk of borrower.

Competition, industry growth

The corporation`s industry level of competition and the growth rate of the industry all factors affect the creditworthiness.

Business risk

Business Risk means uncertainty about the future (of the firm). Business risk of a firm consists of sales risk and operating risk.

Business Model of corporation and market demand

B. *Quantitative Factors*

Ratio analysis is often used for credit analysis. There are three major categories of quantitative factors and their analysis;
    1. Profitability and cash flow
    2. Leverage
    3. Cost of doing business

External factors

There are several external factors like government interferences through monetary and fiscal policies, regulations, GDP level politics and geographical location which affect the borrower's credit worthiness.

2: Calculate and interpret financial ratios used in credit analysis

Ratio analysis is the part of capacity analysis of credit analysis. There are three major categories of ratios in credit analysis;
    1. Profitability and cash flow ratios
    2. Leverage ratios
    3. Coverage ratios

Profitability and cash flow

<u>EBITDA: Earnings before interest, taxes, depreciation, and amortization:</u> This is most commonly metric used to assess the credibility of a company.
<u>EBIT = Operating income + depreciation + amortization</u>

It measures the financial performance of a corporation excluding the effects of depreciation, amortization, taxes and capital expenditures. Exclusion of these costs especially capital expenditures, is the main flaw of ratios which used EBITDA. These expenditures can affect the availability of funds for creditors.

Funds from operations (FFO): It is the net income from continuing operations + amortizations + Depreciation + Deferred tax + other non-cash items. {FFO = EBITDA – changes in working capital}

Free cash flow before dividends: Net income + depreciation + amortization - working capital - capital expenditures. More free flow before dividends better the creditworthiness of company is.

Free cash flow after dividends: This is equal to free cash flow before dividends – dividends

Higher the free cash flow after the dividends means more funds are available for the creditors.

Leverage ratios

Debt to capital ratio = *Total debt / (debt + shareholder's equity)*

It shows the percentage of capital comes from debt. Lower (higher) of this ratio shows higher (lower) creditworthiness and less credit risk. Credit analyst must check if the assets or overvalued to make this ratio attractive especially intangible assets can be easily manipulated. In case of overvaluation the analyst must adjust their values before calculation of this ratio.

Debt to EBITDA = *Total debt /EBITDA:* A higher ratio of this indicated more credit risk. The companies with volatile EBITDA (like seasonal or cyclical industries) have volatile EBITDA so the debt to EBITDA ratio would be highly volatile.

FFO/Debt: Higher of this ratio shows less credit risk.

Free cash flow after dividends/Debt: A higher ratio of this indicated more credit risk.

Coverage ratios

These ratios measure the borrower's ability to pay interest.

EBITDA/Interest expense: Higher of this ratio measures lower credit risk.

EBIT/interest expense: Higher of this ratio measures lower credit risk. This is more conservative approach to EBITDA/interest expense as depreciation and amortization is excluded.

3: Describe the seniority rankings of debt, secured versus unsecured debt and the priority of claims in bankruptcy, and their impact on credit ratings

The debt issued by corporations is ranked with respect to the claims on assets. The debt can be secured (in which there is a specific collateral) and unsecured (in which the lender has general claim on issuer's assets). Debentures are unsecured debts.

Secured debts have higher priority on cash flows from assets than unsecured debts.

The secured debts can be further dived into *first lien or first mortgage, senior secure or second lien and junior secured.* Unsecured debts can also be divided into *Senior, junior and subordinate.* In case of default the claims on unsecured debts are ranked below than secured debt. The claims on debts can be ranked as follows;

1. First lien or first mortgage
2. Senior secured or second lien debt
3. Junior secured debt
4. Senior unsecured debt
5. Senior subordinated debt
6. Subordinated debt
7. Junior subordinated debt

All debts in same category have same priority called *Pari Passu.*

If the firm defaults the first debt that would be paid is first lien or first mortgage and it goes down all the way to last.

This order is theoretically good but sometimes in practice it is very hard to follow this order. The default is very costly and it takes much time to settle. The debt holders (which are not getting 100% of their claims) can agree (off course final decision is may be in hands of court) to reorganization of the seniorities or debt payments. In this case the previous order does not matter and the junior class may get cash before senior class.

LEARNING MODULE 17

Fixed-Income Securitization

1: Explain benefits of securitization for issuers, investors, economies, and financial markets

Securitization: Securitization is a process in which debt instrument like receivables, loans, mortgages etc. are purchased by an entity (called SPE or special purpose entity, special purpose vehicle or special purpose company) and then issues securities backed by those debts. The cash flows on newly issued security are backed by the cash flow from those debt assets (instruments).

Benefits

- The firm selling its financial debt can immediately raises capital to use.
- The backed illiquid financial assets (debts) are now liquid with new security. This new security can be traded in secondary market.
- The credit risk of the firm selling these assets is transferred to new entity.
- A financial company or bank is able to lend more with securitization. Without securitization the bank's lending was limited to traditional assets.
- The investors seeking to invest in debt have more options according to their risk tolerance and return.

Securitization also increases the diversification which reduces risk.

2: Describe securitization, including the parties and the roles they play

Consider L-Corporation which provides autos on installment to its customers. It means the corporation is giving loan to its customers and get installment payments on loan periodically. Suppose it has sold worth $100000 autos to its customers. This $100000 is debt asset for L-corporation. The corporation then establishes a SPE and sells these loans of 100000 to it. The SPE is separate entity from L-corporation. The SPE issues a new security backed by this $100000 and sell to the investors. The newly issued security can be in different classes according to face value, interest rates, payment priorities and claims on assets in case of default. These classes are called *waterfall structure*. The investors have claims on SPE but not on L-corporation. The L-corporation will receive the installments (principal and interest). The L-corporation is the issuer and lender. Issuer and lender can be same or different. S we have following parties with their roll;

Customers: The customers buy autos from L-corporation and pay the amount on installment.

Seller and servicer: The L-Corporation is the seller of autos. It is also the lender who provides loan to these customers but transfers the debt to SPE and receive $100000 from SPE (which is ultimately from investors).

SPE: The organization specially designed for securitization. It will issue debt securities (asset backed securities, ABS) to investors, get the amount and pays to Issuer and lender.

Investors: The investors will receive the periodic interest payment and principal at maturity.

LEARNING MODULE 18

Asset-Backed Security (ABS) Instrument and Market Features

1: Describe characteristics and risks of covered bonds and how they differ from other asset-backed securities

Covered bond: It's a derivative instrument. It is a collection of bank-issued loans, sold to another financial institution for resale. Individual loans in the package stay on the records of the banks who issued them, acting as a collateral pool and providing additional layer to bond holders. Public-sector loans and home loans may be included in the covered bond.
The covered bonds are less risky than ABS, (that's what they are issued for).

Covered bonds vs ABS:

- Covered bonds are similar to asset-backed securities (ABS), but they have two layers: the asset pool and issuing institution.
- Covered bonds are made up of only one type of bond per cover pool. While ABS (credit tranching) is used to create bond classes with varying default exposures.
- The cover pool of a covered bond is continually changing. In contrast to home loans, which are frequently linked with prepayment risk. Covered bond issuers must replace any prepaid or non-performing assets in order to sustain enough cash

flows until maturity.

- Covered bonds are linked to redemption regimes. If the financial sponsor of covered bonds defaults, the redemption regimes ensure that the cash flows closely follow the initial maturity arrangement.

2: Describe typical credit enhancement structures used in securitizations

Typical credit enhancement also called credit tranching or subordination. Newly issued security in securitization can be of single class or multiple classes. In single class all securities are of same credit risk and holders of such securities have equal claims on assets. These different classes of ABS are called tranche. In tranche different classes of ABS holders have different claims on cash flows and the risk is redistributed. Some have more risk than others. Remember total credit risk remains same only redistributed.

Credit tranching/Senior-subordinate structure: Tranching according to credit risk is called credit tranching. In this structure more than one ABS class is issued. One is senior class other is subordinate class A, Subordinate class B and goes on. If an ABS is issued with three classes mentioned above as senior, subordinate A and subordinate B then the subordinate B is of highest risk and also with highest return. If creditor defaults the subordinate B class will lose its money up to a limit. If the loss goes beyond that limit the exceeding loss of principal amount has to bear by subordinate B up to their limit. If that limit also crosses then the senior class will bear that loss. The senior class is least risky (highest in credit rating) so they earn lowest yield.

As each class receives overflow from its senior class in case of liquidation this structure is also called _waterfall structure_.

Time tranching: When ABS are issued with different maturities is called time tranching.

3: Describe types and characteristics of non-mortgage asset-backed securities, including the cash flows and risks of each type

There are some ABS which are not backed by mortgages but by other financial assets like receivables, business loans, credit card receivable loans and home loans etc. these are called non-mortgage asset-backed securities.

Auto loan ABS: ABS backed by auto loans are called auto loan ABS. The cash flow components of these ABS are principal repayments, interest payments and prepayments. These ABS have senior/subordinate structures.

Credit card receivable backed ABS: Securities created from the credit card receivables. The cash flow components of these ABS include finance charges, principal and annual charges. These are non-amortizing loans as the balances on credit cards are revolving. The investors of these ABS are paid periodically but not during lockout period (if any). Interest rate on credit card ABS can be fixed or floating. Sometimes in order to maintain credit quality early (rapid) amortization is required.

4: Describe collateralized debt obligations, including their cash flows and risks

Collateralized debt obligation (CDO) is security backed by debt obligations like corporate and other bonds. CDO is usually issued by SPE and do not rely on interest payment like ABS. The manager of CDOs buys and sells securities to generate promised cash flows to investors. CDOs backed by other CMBS, RMBS, ABS and other CDOs are called structured CDOs. CDOs backed by SWAPS are called synthetic CDOs.

Structure of CDO

SPE issues the CDOs and the manager of CDO buys and sells the debt obligations from CDO pool and generates cash flows. The funds are created by issuing CDOs to investors. These CDOs are also issued in senior/subordinate class.

Risks: Like other securities there are risk of fall in interest rate and default risk. The whole risk is absorbed by the investors of CDOs.

LEARNING MODULE 19

Mortgage-Backed Security (MBS) Instrument and Market Features

1: Define prepayment risk and describe time tranching structures in securitizations and their purpose

There are two types of risks associated with MBS; a decline in interest rate and rise in interest rate. When interest rate declines the clients buy other lower interest loan and pay back the first mortgage before time (prepayments). In this scenario the issuer of mortgage receives fewer revenues as payments of interest rate falls and mortgage maturity reduces. (Also called contraction risk as interest rate falls).

Agency MBS are exposed to a significant prepayment risk as they have no penalty provision for early payment.

Single monthly mortality rate (SMM) is the one way to calculate contraction risk on monthly basis.

$$SMM = \frac{Prepayments\ for\ the\ month}{Begining\ outstanding\ mortgage\ balance - scheduled\ principal\ repayment\ for\ the\ mont}$$

The annualized SMM is called conditional prepayment rate (CPR)
$CPR = (1+SMM)^{(12)} - 1$

A lower SMM and CPR are desirable.

When the interest rate rises the prepayments are less than expectations. Rising interest rate is the opportunity cost of issuer of the mortgage (also called extension risk as interest rate rises).

Time tranching: When ABS are issued with different maturities is called time tranching. Newly issued security in securitization can be of single class or multiple classes. In single class all securities are of same credit risk and holders of such securities have equal claims on assets. These different classes of ABS are called tranche. In tranche different classes of ABS holders have different claims on cash flows and the risk is redistributed. Some have more risk than others. Remember total credit risk remains same only redistributed.

2: Describe fundamental features of residential mortgage loans that are securitized

Residential mortgage: Residential mortgage is a loan by using real estate as collateral. If the borrower defaults the lender has the right to resell the collateral to recover funds. This taking possession back of collateral and reselling is called foreclosure.

The amount of loan is less than the value of property used as collateral. The ratio of loan to value of property is called loan to value ratio. Lower the LTV more the lender is protected.

Two type of mortgage loan usually exist, the prime loan and subprime loan. The prime loan is given to the customers with high credit rating. In prime loan the LTV is higher. Loan with lower LTV is given to the customers with lower credit quality or when the collateral used is being already used in another loan (lower claim of lender on property). This is called subprime loan.

The nature of mortgages differs in different countries. The mortgages can be differentiated with respect to its characteristics like maturity, interest rate determination, amortization schedule, prepayment options and penalties, and foreclosure.

Maturity: This is the duration of loan until complete repayment. The term of a mortgage loan is usually long. In US the usual term of a mortgage falls between 15 to 30 years. In Europe the term can be from 20 to 40 years.

Interest rate determination:

Fixed rate mortgage: This is the mortgage in which the interest rate will remain same during life time of loan.

Variable rate mortgage: In this mortgage the interest rate is adjusted periodically according to the prevailing rate in market or according to some reference like LIBOR. Usually the variable rate mortgage interest rate is given as some spread over LIBOR.

Hybrid mortgage: A mortgage can be with fixed interest rate in its initial stages but after some time it can be a variable mortgage. This is called hybrid mortgage.

Negotiable mortgage: If the interest rate in hybrid mortgage is when changed, fixed to a new interest rate it is called rollover or renegotiable mortgage.

Convertible mortgage: If after some time mortgage is from fixed rate to variable rate (or other way around) for rest of its life with consent of borrower it is called convertible mortgage.

Amortization schedule of principal amount:

Fully amortized loan: With fully amortized mortgage loan the periodic payment include some principal and some interest. When the final payment is made there is no interest or principal amount is left. If the payment amount is fixed, in start the payment includes more interest and less principal which will reverse with passage of time (in later years the payment include less interest and more principal amount.

Partially amortized loan: In this mortgage the periodic payments include some amount of principal and other is interest. The principal amount is not fully amortized during the term of loan. At the end of loan a lump sum of the principal amount is paid.

Interest only or balloon loan: With this mortgage the periodic payments only include the interest and at the end of term the full principal amount is repaid.

Prepayment and penalties:

Prepayments are the partial or full repayments of principal amount by the borrower before time. Sometimes the borrower can find another loan with less interest rate and prepay the first loan from second loan. Mostly the mortgage loan (and other loans too) have a provision of penalty for early payment. This protects the lender in case of decrease in interest rate during term of loan. The penalty is excessive amount over principal amount which the borrower has to pay for early payment.

Foreclosure: In case of default of borrower the lender has the right to take possession of collateral and resell it to generate cash. The value of collateral must be higher than amount of loan. If value of property substantially decreases the borrower can voluntarily give the possession to lender. This is called strategic default. To protect lender from this sometimes the mortgages are recourse loans. In recourse loans the lender has right on borrower equal to the amount of decrease in value of collateral. Recourse loan is common in Europe and is also in use in USA.

3: Describe types and characteristics of residential mortgage-backed securities, including mortgage pass-through securities and collateralized mortgage obligations, and explain the cash flows and risks for each type

The securities issued from securitization of mortgages are called residential mortgage backed securities (RMBS). In USA these securities can be divided into three categories.
1. Federal government guaranteed RMBS (agency RMBS). These are considered to be highest credibility.
2. RMBS guaranteed by government sponsored enterprises (like Fannie Mae and Freddie Mac). These are also considered agency RMBS. Less credibility then first one but still good creditability.
3. RMBS issued by private entities (non agency RMBS). Less credible than above two.

Mortgage pass through securities: When one or more mortgage holders sell share or participation certificates to the pool. The cash flow from collateral pool passes-through to the security holders as coupon and principal payments.

All agency RMBS are pass-through securities. The mortgages are of different maturities so the weighted average maturities (WAM) and weighted average coupon rate (WAC) is applied on pass-through cash flows.

4: Describe characteristics and risks of commercial mortgage-backed securities

Commercial mortgage-backed securities (CMBS) are the securities backed by pool of commercial mortgages. Commercial mortgages are on income producing properties (real estate). These real estates can be multi-family apartments, warehouses, office buildings, shopping centers etc. The CMBS are repaid by investors of these properties while the residential MBS are repaid by the homeowners.

Credit risk: The CMBS are concourse loans as the lender has only claim on the commercial properties and not on other assets. This is the reason the credit risk of CMBS is only attached with market value of property (not with the borrower of the loan). Two ratios are considered to calculate credit risk of CMBS; the debt-to-service coverage ratio (debt coverage ratio) and loan-to-value ratio.

Debt-to-service coverage ratio = $\frac{Net\ operating\ income}{Debt\ service}$

Net operating income = income from property – property taxes
Debt service = Principal repayments and interest payments

Higher of this ratio shows less risk as income is sufficiently being generated from property.

Loan to value ratio = $\frac{Current\ mortgage\ amount}{current\ appraised\ value\ of\ propert}$

Appraised value of the property is the value which is determined by lender (not by market). Usually it is the value which will be received when property is sold immediately.

Lower of this ratio is desirable for lender. This ratio shows how many times current amount of the mortgage can be paid with the property value.

Structure

Credit rating agencies asses the credit risk of CMBS. These CMBS are structured in tranches and lowest priority tranche is usually excluded in credit risk calculation.

CMBS usually have call provision which protects investors against prepayments. There are two types of call protection
Loan level call protection and CMBS structure call protection.

Loan level call protection: This call protection can be in any one of four ways.

Prepayment lockout: This provision restricts the borrower from prepayment for a specific period.

Defeasance: In this the borrower put some funds or portfolio of lowest risk (or high credibility) to repay the principal and or interest amount.

Prepayment penalty point: Points are fixed as penalty for early payments. Each point represents 1% of principal prepayment.

Yield maintenance charges: In this provision the charges are paid equivalent to the lender's loss of interest rate. This makes the borrower and lender indifferent of weather to pay early or not.

All these penalties are distributed in investors according to the structure of CMBS.

CMBS structure call protection:
In this the CBMS is divided into different tranches (higher priority and lower priority) and different call provisions are applied to different tranches.

Mostly the CMBS are structured in a way that the borrower has to pay huge amount at the end of term of loan term. This is called *balloon payment*. The risk attached with balloon payment is called *balloon risk.* If the borrower defaults the lender is require to extend the period of loan. This extended period is called *workout period*. Interest rate is higher in workout period because no default risk is also attached.

www.ingramcontent.com/pod-product-compliance
Lightning Source LLC
Chambersburg PA
CBHW070358230526
45471CB00006B/2624